CHILDREN LIKE US
Transportation
AROUND THE WORLD

Moira Butterfield

Cavendish
Square

New York

Published in 2016 by Cavendish Square Publishing, LLC
243 5th Avenue, Suite 136, New York, NY 10016

Cataloging-in-Publication Data

Butterfield, Moira.
Transportation around the world / by Moira Butterfield.
p. cm. — (Children like us)
Includes index.
ISBN 978-1-5026-0856-7 (hardcover) ISBN 978-1-5026-0854-3 (paperback) ISBN 978-1-5026-0857-4 (ebook)
1. Transportation — Juvenile literature. I. Butterfield, Moira, 1960-. II. Title.
TA1149.B88 2016
388—d23

Editor: Izzi Howell
Designer: Clare Nicholas
Picture researcher: Izzi Howell
Wayland editor: Annabel Stones

Picture credits:
The author and publisher would like to thank the following for allowing their pictures to be reproduced in this publication: cover Bartosz Hadyniak/Getty Images; p.3 (t-b) Tooykrub/Shutterstock, mofles/iStock, Faiz Zaki/Shutterstock, bluecrayola/Shutterstock; pp.4-5 (c) ekler/Shutterstock; p.4 (t) carterdayne/iStock, (b) Bartosz Hadyniak/iStock; p.5 (tl) Forster Forest/Shutterstock, (tr) Tooykrub/Shutterstock, (b) Faiz Zaki/Shutterstock; p.6 (t) danm12/Shutterstock, (bl) Bufflerump/Shutterstock, (br) TravnikovStudio/Shutterstock; p.7 DC_Colombia/iStock; p.8 (t) Duc Den Thui/Shutterstock, (c) Christian Vinces/Shutterstock, (b) Bartosz Hadyniak/iStock; p.9 Bartosz Hadyniak/iStock; p.10 Hamid Sardar/Corbis; p.11 (t) Roberto A Sanchez/iStock, (b) Forster Forest/Shutterstock; p.12 (t) jiratto/Shutterstock, (c) Fritz Hoffmann/In Pictures/Corbis, (b) Chor Sokunthea/Reuters/Corbis; p.13 Leonid Andronov/Shutterstock; p.14 (t) efesenko/iStock, (b) Al Satterwhite/Transtock/Corbis; p.15 (l) urosr/Shutterstock, (r) Daniel M. Nagy/Shutterstock; p.16 (t) bodrumsurf/iStock, (b) Ronnie Kaufman/Larry Hirshowitz/Blend Images/Corbis; p.17 (t) Flavio Vallenari/iStock, (b) SerrNovik/iStock; p.18 (t) Luca Zanon/XianPix/Corbis, (b) m.bonotto/Shutterstock; p.19 topten22photo/Shutterstock; p.20 Tooykrub/Shutterstock; p.21 (t) Paul Thompson/Eye Ubiquitous/Corbis, (b) mofles/iStock; p. 22 (t) Volodymyr Kyrylyuk/Shutterstock, (c) R McIntyre/Shutterstock, (b) Steven Georges/Press-Telegram/Corbis; p.23 carterdayne/iStock; p.24 (t) bluecrayola/Shutterstock, (c) bluecrayola/Shutterstock, (b) PhotoStock10/Shutterstock; p.25 MarcelClemens/Shutterstock; p.26 kylieellway/iStock, (b) Pichugin Dmitry/Shutterstock; p.27 Faiz Zaki/Shutterstock; p.28 (t) paintings/Shutterstock, (b) Ivan Cholakov/iStock; p.29 Fredrik Von Erichson/epa/Corbis; p.30 (l-r, t-b) Bartosz Hadyniak/iStock, Mlenny/iStock, Forster Forest/Shutterstock, Tooykrub/Shutterstock, LUNAMARINA/iStock, PhotoStock10/Shutterstock, TravnikovStudio/Shutterstock, Cristi Lucaci/Shutterstock, Duc Den Thui/Shutterstock, Natali Glado/Shutterstock, bluecrayola/Shutterstock, danm12/Shutterstock, vorakorn/Shutterstock, efesenko/iStock, p.31 (l) Ronnie Kaufman/Larry Hirshowitz/Blend Images/Corbis, (r) Fredrik Von Erichson/epa/Corbis.

Design elements used throughout: philia/Shutterstock, rassco/Shutterstock, lilac/Shutterstock, DVARG/Shutterstock, Studio Barcelona/Shutterstock, Dacian G/Shutterstock, Juampi Rodriguez/Shutterstock, Bimbim/Shutterstock, Tribalium/Shutterstock, Alexey V Smirnov/Shutterstock, Crystal Eye Studio/Shutterstock, JSlavy/Shutterstock, ElenaShow/Shutterstock, antoninaart/Shutterstock, mhatzapa/Shutterstock, snapgalleria/Shutterstock, Anton Lunkov/Shutterstock, eatcute/Shutterstock, sarahdesign/Shutterstock, Mascha Tace/Shutterstock, NorSob/Shutterstock.

Printed in the United States of America

Contents

Getting Around

Are you ready to find out how children around the world get around? You'll find out how people get across deserts and over mountains. You'll see trains, planes, boats, and horse-drawn carts.

What makes this American hot air balloon rise into the sky? Find out on page 23.

Boats allow us to get across lakes and rivers. Find out what this Peruvian girl's boat is made from on page 8.

Skiing is a way to move across the snow. Learn why this Norwegian boy is skiing with poles on page 11.

Find out why horses are so important to these Mongolian boys on page 20.

Why do you think these Malaysian three-wheeled bikes are decorated with flowers? Find out why on page 27.

Take a trip around the world to see the transportion used by children just like you!

Cross a City

Every day, around 150,000 cars, trucks, buses, and bicycles drive around the Indian city of Delhi. They share the roads with much older and slower types of transportation, too. Some people travel in ox-pulled carts.

This ox cart is delivering sacks of grain around Delhi.

Taxis of all kinds criss-cross the world's cities. The taxis in New York have been painted yellow for over one hundred years. People can easily recognize them and hail them in the street.

Official taxi cabs in New York have to be painted yellow by law.

This young New Yorker is hailing a city taxi. She puts her arm out to ask to the taxi driver to stop.

The three cable car lines in La Paz match the country flag. They are red, green, and yellow.

You can take a cable car ride high above the traffic in La Paz, Bolivia. The city's cable cars are the highest in the world. They are around 2.5 miles (3,962 m) above sea level. The cable car system is also the longest in the world.

Ride on Water

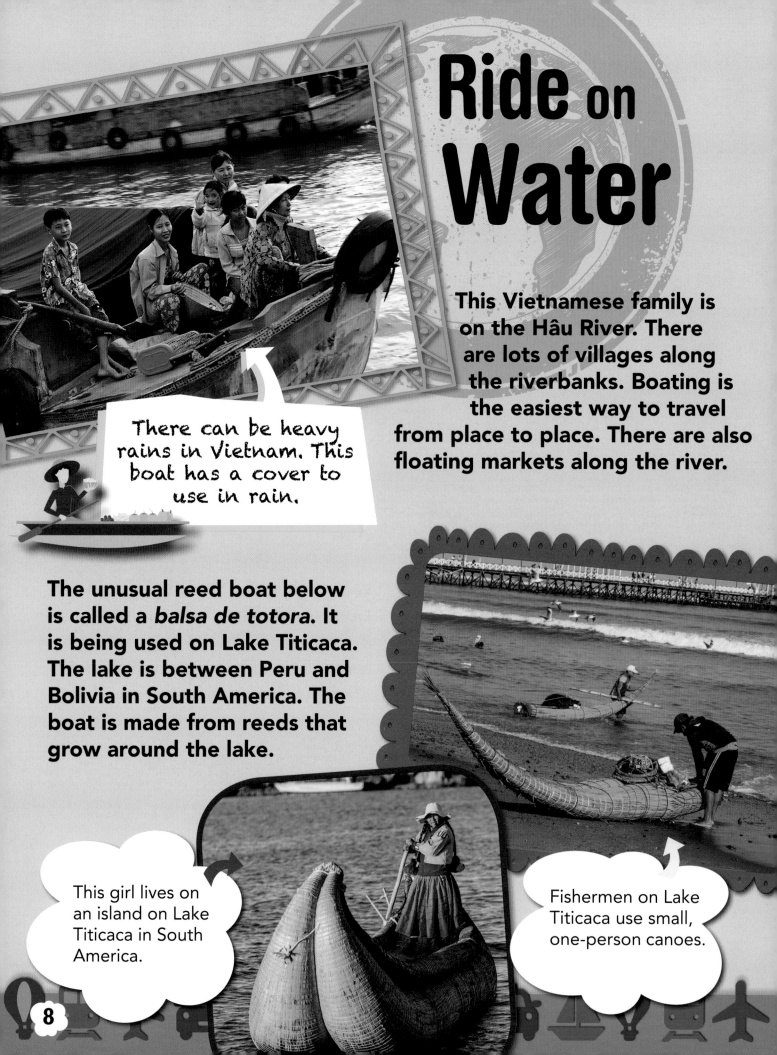

This Vietnamese family is on the Hâu River. There are lots of villages along the riverbanks. Boating is the easiest way to travel from place to place. There are also floating markets along the river.

There can be heavy rains in Vietnam. This boat has a cover to use in rain.

The unusual reed boat below is called a *balsa de totora*. It is being used on Lake Titicaca. The lake is between Peru and Bolivia in South America. The boat is made from reeds that grow around the lake.

This girl lives on an island on Lake Titicaca in South America.

Fishermen on Lake Titicaca use small, one-person canoes.

These Sri Lankan boys use oars to move their boat.

These boys paddle their hollowed-out log canoe on the Maduganga River in Sri Lanka. Their home is in a swampy wetland area. It is hard to build roads across the boggy ground. The best way to get around is by boat.

Through the Snow

Dukha children travel around with their family, herding reindeer.

In very cold places, people need special ways to get through the snow. The Dukha tribe live in northern Mongolia. They look after herds of reindeer. They choose the strongest ones to ride across the snow.

Snowmobiles are great for getting around in snow. Snowmobiles have tracks instead of wheels. This lets them drive in deep snow. Plus, they can carry one or two people.

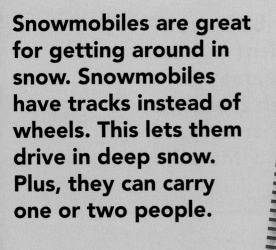

Skis fitted to a snowmobile help it slide over snow.

In snowy countries, everybody learns to ski from an early age. There are two types of skiing. There is fast downhill skiing. There is also cross-country skiing.

This Norwegian boy is cross-country skiing. The poles help him move forward.

Take to the Tracks

This bullet train zooms past Mount Fuji in Japan.

The world's fastest train system is the Shinkansen. It runs across Japan. The trains are nicknamed "bullet trains" because they are so fast. The record for the fastest train of all goes to the Japanese-designed Maglev train. It can travel at over 373 miles per hour (600 kph).

Maglev trains use electric-powered magnets to hover above the track. This Maglev train connects Shanghai city center to the airport.

This crowded Cambodian bamboo train is called a *nori*. It is a platform made from bamboo slats. It has been fitted with a small engine. It travels down the tracks at about 9 mph (15 kph).

Bamboo railways ferry people between villages in Batambang, Cambodia.

Some children that run the Children's Railway will work on the railways when they leave school.

The Children's Railway in Kiev, Ukraine, is run by children. There were once many Children's Railways of this kind. They were built to give schoolchildren the chance to train for jobs.

Explore a Desert

These quad bikers are riding through the Sahara in North Africa. A quad bike is a good way to drive on soft sand. Its four big wheels spread out its weight. This way, it doesn't sink and get stuck.

Sand can sting when it hits your skin. These quad bikers have covered their faces with scarves.

This boy and his dad are riding in a dune buggy in Baja, California. Dune buggies are raced across the beaches in this area. They have big, wide tires. The engine is in the back to weigh down the light buggy as it zips over the dunes.

Dune buggies don't have any windows. This boy is keeping his face safe with goggles.

This Ethiopian girl guides her camel using the string wrapped around its head.

For centuries, people have ridden camels across Middle Eastern and African deserts. This girl lives in the deserts of Ethiopia. Her camel has wide padded feet that keep it from sinking into the soft sand. Its coat keeps it cool in hot weather and warm on chilly nights.

Camels have three eyelids and two sets of eyelashes to keep sand out of their eyes.

Up a **Mountain**

Donkeys are great at carrying things up mountains. They are strong and good at keeping their footing on rocky paths. This donkey is working in the Himalayas. It's the world's highest mountain range.

This Himalayan donkey has bells attached to his harness. This lets the owner hear where it is.

Mountain bikes are good for riding on bumpy off-road tracks.

Today, mountain bikes are used everywhere. They were invented in the late 1970s in California. At that time, some people said they would never catch on! They have a strong frame and tough tires, which are just right for cycling down rocky paths.

This man takes in summer views from a chairlift at Mount Balo in the Italian Alps.

This chairlift is on the ski slopes of Colorado, USA.

Chairlifts travel up and down mountainsides on cables. They can give passengers a great view in summer. Plus, they take them to hard-to-reach ski slopes in winter.

Around the Festival

The rowers in Regata Storica dress in uniforms like those once worn by the servants of rich Venetian nobles.

Every September, the canals of Venice, Italy, fill with a parade of historic boats. It is called the Regata Storica. Crowds line the waterways to see the beautiful gondolas and barges. The festival dates back around five hundred years.

Carnival floats can help to raise money for charity. People throw money onto the floats they like best.

Parades are held around the world at festival times. Some parades have incredible decorated floats for these events. These floats are from the Viareggio Carnival. It is held in Italy every February at the start of the Christian festival of Lent.

Elephants provide the transportation at the Buat Chang celebration. This parade takes place in Thailand. It celebrates boys who have been accepted to train as Buddhist monks. They dress up and ride on elephants through town.

In the Buat Chang parade, the elephants are painted in colorful patterns.

All Kinds of Horses

Horses have been used as transportation for thousands of years. In Mongolia, they are still very important. Nearly every family has horses. They use horses for riding and to carry things. Female horses are kept for their milk. It is made into the popular Mongolian drink, *kumis*.

Horses are so important in Mongolia that there is a famous saying: "A Mongolian without a horse is like a bird without wings."

These children are riding an Andalucian horse in Seville, Spain. Andalucian horses are highly prized. At the Feria de Abril, a spring fair, people parade through the city with their finest Andalucian horses.

Many riders dress in traditional clothing at the Feria de Abril.

This Mennonite family used modern materials to make a traditional horse-drawn buggy.

These children are from a Mennonite community in Yucatán, Mexico. Mennonite people do not use modern transportation. Instead, they use horse-drawn buggies.

Take to the Air

Seaplanes can land directly on water or ice. They have ski-style floats, which keep them from sinking. Seaplanes are useful for reaching lakes and rivers in places that don't have roads.

People commute from Vancouver to Victoria, Canada, using seaplanes.

This seaplane is landing on a lake in the United States.

This boy is flying over Long Beach in California, USA. He is not in an airplane, though. He is in a blimp, which is like a giant balloon full of gas. He is riding with the pilot.

Gas keeps the blimp in the air. There is an engine and other parts to steer it, too.

Look closely. Do you see people riding in the basket under this hot air balloon? It floats because it is filled with hot air. Air is heated by a burner beneath the balloon. Hot air is lighter than cool air, so it rises.

There is a big hot air balloon festival in New Mexico, USA, every year.

Win a Race

These children are racing in a soapbox derby in Kiel, Germany. Soapbox derby cars were once made out of large wooden crates used to store soap. Soapbox derby cars do not have engines. The race course must be downhill.

Soapbox derby cars are made at home using recycled equipment.

Lots of children make themed soapbox derby cars.

Go-karts come in different shapes and sizes.

Many of the world's top race car drivers started racing when they were children. They started in junior go-kart races. A go-kart has four wheels. It is open on top. It has an engine and gears.

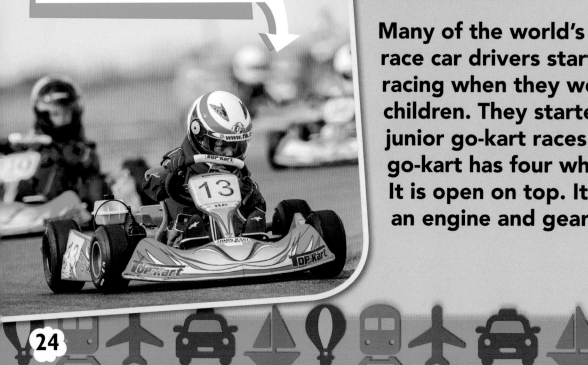

BMX races are contests between BMX bicycle riders. BMX tracks are built with lots of bumps. Races take less than a minute, but they are action-packed. These young riders are competing at a BMX race in Verona, Italy.

A BMX bike has a light, strong frame. This makes it great for fast racing over bumpy ground.

Fancy Transportation

This *camioneta* bus carries passengers around Guatemala, Central America. This bus started out as a school bus in the USA or Canada. Once it got to Guatemala, it got some colorful new decorations.

Each *camioneta* bus is painted differently. Their drivers are very proud of them. They are works of art on wheels!

In Pakistan, truck drivers make their trucks their own with paint, mirrors, tassels, and carved pieces of wood. These vehicles are sometimes called "jingle trucks." This is because they can have chimes that jingle as the truck drives.

Pakistani drivers spend lots of money trying to make their trucks look extra fancy.

These children are riding in a bicycle taxi called a trishaw. It takes them through the streets of Malacca, Malaysia. The trishaw is decorated with flowers to draw in customers. Every trishaw is decorated differently.

Tourists love the trishaws in Malacca.

Amazing Transportation

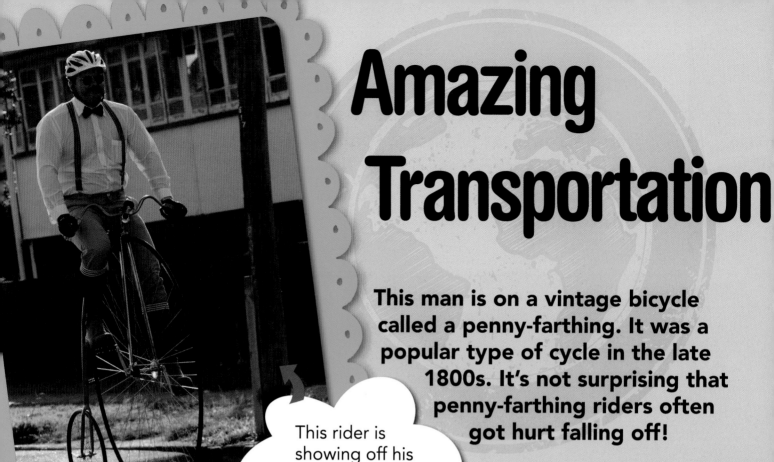

This man is on a vintage bicycle called a penny-farthing. It was a popular type of cycle in the late 1800s. It's not surprising that penny-farthing riders often got hurt falling off!

This rider is showing off his penny-farthing in Brisbane, Australia.

This car is a "weinermobile." It is one of the most famous unusual vehicles in the United States. This one has been made for a company to advertise hot dogs. It is driven to events around the country.

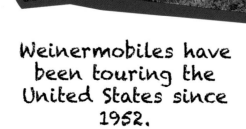

Weinermobiles have been touring the United States since 1952.

This amphibious car model is an Amphicar. It was first made in the 1960s.

Is this a car or is it a boat? It's both! It's an amphibious car. This means it can drive on land or in water. It's taking a trip on the River Mosel in Germany. There are many other amphibious vehicles besides cars.

Art Station

Here are some ideas for getting creative and designing your own world!

- Design your own boat. Label its special features and give it a name. Where would you sail your boat— on lakes, rivers or the ocean?

- Design a crazy kind of car, like the cars on pages 28 and 29. Label the features of your invention.

- Design some art to go on the side of a bus or a truck. It could be a picture or it could include some words.

- Draw a carnival float that you would like to build for a parade. What is the parade celebrating?

Glossary

amphibious Something that can travel on land and in water.

Andalucian From Andalucia, a part of southern Spain.

blimp A name for an airship, a floating balloon vehicle.

Buddhist Someone who believes in the religion of Buddhism.

cable car A passenger carriage that hangs from cables.

chairlift A chair pulled up and down a slope on cables.

customize Change to make something look different.

gondola A rowing boat used in Venice, Italy, or the passenger cabin of a blimp (airship).

harness Leather straps fitted on a horse or donkey to help it pull a cart or carry loads.

Mennonites A group of people who believe in a particular kind of Christianity.

novice Beginner.

quad bike A motorbike with four large wheels.

trishaw A bicycle taxi with a seat for a passenger on the side.

vintage A design from the past.

wetland A region which is swampy and criss-crossed by streams.

Further Information

Websites

Public Transportation (NatGeo Education)
National Geographic provides an in-depth look at popular modes of transportation.
education.nationalgeographic.com/media/public-transportation-geostory/

Transport
A look at the transportation in India.
www.oddizzi.com/teachers/explore-the-world/country-close-up/case-study-india/living-in-india/transport-2/

Transportation
An informative look at transportation around the world.
easyscienceforkids.com/all-about-transportation/

Books

Lyons, Shelly. *Transportation in My Neighborhood*. North Mankato, WI: Capstone Press, 2013.

Morganelli, Adrianna. *Transportation in Different Places*. New York, NY: Crabtree Publishing Company, 2015.

Rustad, Martha E.H. *Transportation in Many Cultures*. North Mankato, WI: Capstone Press, 2011.

Index